The Usborne

CREATIVE WRITER'S HANDBOOK

With lots of note pages at the back for your own ideas and stories.

Contents

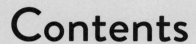
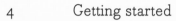

Not sure what to write about? This section is for you!

Use these pages to fine-tune your story writing techniques.

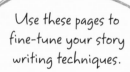

Brush up on basic rules and be inspired by some varied vocabulary.

Getting started

Putting words on a page is easy. The harder part of being a creative writer is knowing which words to choose and how to use them. That's where this book comes in...

Basic tools

All you need to start writing is a pen or pencil and some paper!

Carry a notebook when you're out and about.

Roald Dahl liked to write in pencil on yellow paper. He didn't mind ~~scribbling~~ crossing things out to make his stories better.

or adding things in

Useful eraser

Increasingly, writers are using phones and tablets to make notes, and computers for their final writing.

There are 14 pages for your own writing at the back of this book.

Turn to page 95.

Make sure you can read your writing, but don't make it so neat that you're afraid to cross things out.

My posh pen

What to write

Flick through the different sections in this book for inspiration, or use the index on page 110 to look up specific areas of writing.

How to write

Creative writing is about... being creative. Use the processes and techniques described in this book to develop your own, unique writing style.

Who wrote it

Quotations throughout the book show different writing techniques in action.

> In a hole in the ground there lived a hobbit.
>
> [From *The Hobbit* by J. R. R. Tolkein]

The author's name and where the quote is from are written like this.

Where to write

Ideally, you want to find a quiet, comfortable writing place, where you won't be interrupted. A corner of your bedroom might be a good place to start.

The Welsh poet Dylan Thomas wrote from a bike shed perched on stilts on a cliff.

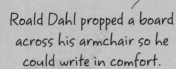

J. K. Rowling wrote her first books sitting in a café.

Roald Dahl propped a board across his armchair so he could write in comfort.

Extra tools

Look out for these devices in the book.

> Ovals are for interesting captions.

Top tips
These circles give snippets of excellent advice.

Arrows suggest which pages you might like to turn to next.

Internet links symbol

Internet links

Each time you see the internet links symbol, it means you can find links to recommended websites at the Usborne Quicklinks website. Turn to page 112 for more information.

GHOSTLY GALLEON REACHES NEW YORK

How I felt...

Robots rule

Ideas

A hidden message

If animals could talk...

BEST DANCER

Inspiration from others

To write well, it helps to read LOTS. See what other writers write. The more you read, the more you can build up your writing skills.

Read anything

Don't just read the books you know you like. Try ones you're less sure about. They can all help you to develop your own writing style.

There's some interesting vocabulary in here!

Comedy

Historical novel

Play script

Detective story

Science fiction

Biography

DIY MANUAL

Graphic novel

Elizabethan poetry

Zombies

Recipe book

Japanese Haiku

How do you develop a plot by using dialogue?

How do people write about real lives?

Be discerning

Not everything you read is going to be well written. Ask yourself what makes some books so captivating and others yawn-inducingly dull.

I love this book because

* I really care about the main character.
* It transports me to another place.
* It expresses exactly how I feel.
* The ending is totally unexpected.

There are word lists to inspire your writing on pages 84-91.

Be a collector

Collect quotations that have caught your eye, and learn passages by heart. Surround yourself with words and ideas that will inspire your own writing.

We are all in the gutter, but some of us are looking at the stars.

[From *Lady Windermere's Fan* by Oscar Wilde]

I'm terrified that my journey won't tie up all the loose ends nicely. Because this is a life, not just a story, and life doesn't always go the way stories tell you.

[From *The Manifesto on How to be Interesting* by Holly Bourne]

Find your own voice

Imitating other writers can help you to explore different styles, but ultimately you need to develop your own way of writing.

Learn new words

Reading widens your vocabulary. That doesn't mean you have to use longer words, but you will have a wider selection to choose from.

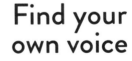

Learn a new word a day via the Usborne Quicklinks website.

angle   catch   haul   flounder   reel   fish   trawl   cast

9

Everyday ideas

Ideas for stories are all around you.
You just need to be alert to them.

Find more story
starters via the Usborne
Quicklinks website.

Unusual happenings

Look out for anything unusual – and make up a
surprising explanation as a starting point for a story.

A street named 'Hanging Sword Alley'
– Why? What happened here?

The only run-down house on a very
smart avenue – Who lives in it?

A scratching sound coming from the
kitchen cupboard – What is it?

An eccentric inventor
has managed to teleport
himself and his house
into a much posher
neighbourhood.

Ordinary objects

Every object has a story to tell – or a past you can invent about it.

Granny's sugar bowl

Once held the
false teeth of an
American president.

The old oak
tree in the park

Used to be a hide-out
for Robin Hood.

A chocolate wrapper

Deliberately discarded
by a spy – contains
a secret code.

Get tips for writing dialogue
on pages 42-43.

Conversation snippets

An overheard comment could be just the spark
you need for a story.

He didn't turn up for
his own funeral.

Faked his own death?
Why? Double life?

There was peanut butter
all over the dog.

A crazy invention
gone wrong?

The giraffe
arrives tonight.

Code name for a
secret consignment?

Where to hear snippets

- Supermarket check-outs
- Cafés
- Public transport
- Park benches
- Public cubicles, e.g. at
  the swimming pool
- Playgrounds

Where to watch people

- Town squares
- Shopping malls
- Libraries
- Large family occasions
- Train and bus stations
- Airports

People watching

Most stories are built around individual characters. Look out for
a curious action or interaction that might be the start of a story.

What are they
arguing about?

A joyful reunion –
who's been where?

Who's the plant
for and why?

11

In the news

Search the local, national or international news for a topical idea to write about.

NEWS CHOICE

ICEBERG THREATENS TOWN

The Local Paper

SCHOOL WINS LOTTERY

Global Headlines

PRIME MINISTER EXPLODES IN TANTRUM

Daily Herald

ESCAPED PANDA EATS GARDEN FENCE

An unusual advertisement might catch your eye.

FOR SALE:
ENGAGEMENT RING, NEARLY NEW

See what's in the news via the Usborne Quicklinks website.

Fact to fiction

Use a headline or news story as a starting point, then flesh it out with your own characters and plot twists.

> Inhabitants of the peaceful town of Izelthump have only two hours to protect themselves from the world's largest iceberg.
>
> How?
> Blow it up? Melt it?
> Tow it away?

Pick and mix

You could pick characters and ideas from different news items, and see what story you can make when you put them together.

ESCAPED PANDA **WINS LOTTERY**

Old news

It doesn't have to be a recent news article. Search the internet or your local library for an old news story. It might inspire a fascinating historical novel...

Ye Olde News
TITANIC SINKS

From experience

Find inspiration from your own life. It's easier to write convincingly about something you've experienced first hand.

Make it real

Try to recapture the moment as it happened, so a reader can experience it in a similar way to you.

- Set the scene.
- Describe what was going through your mind.
- Create tension.

Include smells and sounds as well as things you see.

At the time, you didn't know what would happen next.

In disguise

Sometimes it's easier and less embarrassing to dress up a personal experience as fiction.

- Write in the third person ('he' or 'she', not 'I').
- Use a different name.
- Change the location and any other details that reveal your identity.

An experience doesn't need to be dramatic to be worth writing about. Try describing the way something made you feel.

That taste instantly transported me back to my childhood...

Two sides to a story

Remember – what you did, said and how you felt is only one version of events...

The Failed Actress

As I took my final bow, blissfully unaware of my skirt caught in my knickers, the spontaneous applause made me beam with pride. Only afterwards did I realize they were merely clapping out of sympathy.

Hopes and dreams

The stuff of dreams can provide an excellent starting point for a story. Explore your own dreams and ambitions for ideas.

World champion

How would it feel to really excel at a sport or hobby you love? Plan a story that takes you all the way to the top.

Trampolining

- From a hobby in the backyard... to a gold medal at the Olympics!
- Add some injury, rivalry and disappointment along the way.

Winning the lottery

£1,000,000

Imagine picking the winning numbers and becoming a millionaire over night.

What would you do with the money?

How would things be different?

Life saver

Could your amazing ideas or daring actions help others?

Perhaps you could...

...find a new source of antibiotics in the Amazon rainforest.

...foil a terrorist bomb plot.

...rescue an endangered species from extinction.

More dream ideas

- Being elected Prime Minister or President
- Playing the leading role in a Hollywood blockbuster
- Travelling the world in a hot air balloon
- Finding a cure for cancer
- Breaking the land speed record in a supersonic car

What if?

Imagine an alternative reality. What strange scenarios might happen? Would they make a good story?

Change the rules

Take an everyday situation and turn it on its head.

> What if...
>
> ...the students became the teachers?
>
> ...the sun only rose once a month?
>
> ...animals could talk?

Science fiction

Think how a scientific discovery or an advance in technology might change where and how we live.

- Space exploration?
- Super powers?
- Time travel?

Parallel universe

Perhaps ours isn't the only universe out there. Other worlds might exist, vastly different or uncannily similar.

- Your character finds a doorway or portal to another world.
- It's the same as Earth, except people walk on their hands, not their feet.

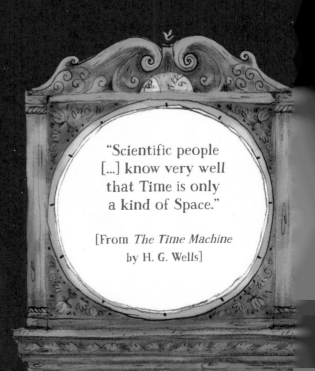

"Scientific people [...] know very well that Time is only a kind of Space."

[From *The Time Machine* by H. G. Wells]

Planning

Summary

Sum up your story idea before you develop the details.
It helps you to keep track of where you're heading.

Brainstorm

Ask yourself key questions about your story... and check you know the answers! Here are questions and answers for a story about Robin Hood as an example.

Who?

- Robin Hood
- His merry band of outlaws
- The sheriff of Nottingham

Where?

- Sherwood Forest
- Nottingham town
- The sheriff's castle

What?

- The sheriff organizes an archery competition.
- Robin goes in disguise and wins the golden arrow prize.
- Robin taunts the sheriff with a victory note.

When?

- Hundreds of years ago
- Don't be too specific; keep it timeless.

Why?

- The sheriff and Robin are sworn enemies.
- The sheriff wants to trap Robin.
- Robin can't resist a challenge and a chance to annoy the sheriff.

How?

Details of *how* the action unfolds can come later, once you've got a good overview of the story.

Join up the answers

Piece together the essentials of your story to make a summary that's short and clear.

Just state the basic facts, in order.

Dialogue and description can be developed later.

Don't worry about giving the ending away. This is a summary, not a back cover blurb.

ROBIN & THE GOLDEN ARROW - A SUMMARY

It's a long time ago in Nottingham castle. An evil sheriff hatches a plot to trap his arch enemy, Robin. He announces an archery contest, with a golden arrow as a prize.

News of the contest reaches the outlaws in Sherwood Forest. Against his merry men's advice, Robin enters the contest - disguised as a beggar.

As the sheriff searches the crowd for Robin, the 'beggar' fires his way into the final round of the competition and clinches the prize.

That evening, Robin fires the golden arrow through the sheriff's window, with a signed note of thanks. The sheriff is furious!

Mix it up

Try writing a summary of a story you know well, then change the characters and setting and see what happens!

Summaries are usually written in the present tense, even if your story takes place in the past.

For ideas on developing your settings and characters, turn to pages 28-31.

Mind map

Mind maps help you to gather your thoughts before you begin writing. Put your topic in the middle, then develop a web of ideas around it.

Here's a mind map for a story based on a Greek myth, where two prisoners plot their escape...

Main characters

The prisoners, Icarus and his dad Daedalus

Impulsive
Moody
Frustrated at being cooped up in the tower prison

Genius
Eccentric
Feels responsible for their imprisonment

Other characters

Evil King Minos

Soldiers guarding the tower

Theseus (backstory)

The seagulls!

Icarus – the boy who flew too high

Seagulls as inspiration for escape plan? Bribe them with bread for their feathers?

Plot

Build-up
Daedalus comes up with a daring plan to escape the tower. It takes months to collect enough feathers to make wings, which they stick together with candle wax.

Climax
Icarus and Daedalus launch from the tower. They can fly! But foolish Icarus flies too close to the sun. His wings melt... and he's never seen again.

Read more Greek myths via the Usborne Quicklinks website.

Ideas tip

Use a mind map to brainstorm any writing ideas, from a report or a rap to a novel or a documentary.

Setting

Island of Crete

Tower inside the labyrinth

Surrounded by Mediterranean Sea

Hot and dry
Rugged mountains
Gnarled olive trees
Lots of goats

Impossible to escape...

The labyrinth is the most complicated maze ever designed.

What to add

Headings

Try to group ideas under headings, to help order your thoughts. Choose any headings you like to suit your topic.

Links

Use arrows or lines to link up ideas and show how they relate to each other.

Timeline

Backstory
Daedalus designed the labyrinth for King Minos, then angered the king by helping Theseus to escape.

Main story
How they plan and execute their escape

Not shown
Minos's reaction to the escape and Icarus's final moments

More ideas

Your map can become as big and busy as you like, with more and more ideas stemming from the ones you already have.

Doodles

Sometimes it's easier to doodle an idea rather than write it down. Both methods work well on a mind map.

Daedalus just sees a floating pile of feathers.

Story mountain

There are many different ways to plan out a story. A story mountain is a useful place to start, particularly with shorter stories.

Setting off

Who do you need to introduce in the **beginning**?

Where are they?

What are they doing?

The ascent

Develop the problem, the intrigue, the tension, the **build-up**.

Beware! Yeti!

The journey

Your characters need to get from the beginning of your story to the end, but on the way there's a massive mountain to climb.

That mountain is the problem, predicament or challenge at the heart of your story.

Added danger

You can always add in extra complications and unexpected hurdles.

You can also plan a story backwards – see page 27.

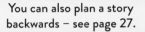

Scaling the top

This is the dramatic **climax** where things could go irreversibly wrong. It's make or break. Add lots of suspense.

The descent

Your characters are over the worst, but there are still some misunderstandings to clear up or some problems that need a **resolution**.

Print out story mountain templates via the Usborne Quicklinks website.

They've made it!

Or have they? Is everyone still in one piece? Will things ever be the same again? What makes a good **ending**?

Story tip

Introduce new characters along the way, to help or hinder the main characters.

Plot devices

Plot devices are elements that move a story on.
They should link seamlessly within a story.

A framing device

A story told within the context of another story.

The Arabian Nights stories, including Aladdin and Ali Baba, are told within the framework of a Sultan's wife telling stories to entertain her husband.

A discovery

A sudden realization of how characters are related or how events are linked.

Anonymous letter?

Old photograph?

An object of power

The hero needs to find this object before the villain does, or else...

The key to the lost treasure?

The missing formula?

A narrative hook

This is a way to draw the reader in and catch their attention.

A dramatic opener

A curious statement

A chase scene

Exciting action, used to heighten tension.

Car chase?

Over the rooftops?

Dangling from a helicopter?

A cliffhanger

An abrupt ending to a chapter or episode that leaves the audience desperate to know what happens next.

Will Aladdin ever escape the cave?

Will the 40 ruthless thieves find Ali Baba?

Will Sinbad be rescued from the valley of man-eating snakes?

A reversal

The circumstances are turned on their head.

Cinderella's stepsisters end up in rags.

A twist

An unexpected turn of events, often near the end.

The hero is the villain's father!

It was all a dream.

A red herring

Something or someone that deflects attention from the real action or facts of a situation.

A forged document?

In the wrong place at the wrong time?

Tent pole events

Longer stories tend to have more than one main plot event. You could think of the story as a tent and the events as tent poles.

Tent tip
The bigger the tent, the more poles it will need!

Creating structure

Key events help to shape a narrative, give it structure and keep readers interested.

Make sure your events are all somehow linked to the main storyline.

Three acts

Each tent pole event could be a different act in a play. Many dramas are planned in three acts:

Act 1
Setting up the story

Antonio, the tightrope artist, is chosen for the main circus act.

His rival, Barry, is seething with jealousy.

Act 2
The main confrontation

A sudden noise causes Antonio to fall and break his leg.

Barry takes over as lead performer, under a cloud of suspicion.

Act 3
The resolution

The sudden noise has an innocent explanation.

Antonio recovers from his broken leg.

Barry and Antonio become a famous double act.

Reverse planning

If you have a strong idea of how your story will finish, it might help to start at the end and work back.

Let's look at *The Wizard of Oz* as an example.

"And oh, Aunt Em! I'm so glad to be home again!"

[The last line in *The Wizard of Oz*, by L. Frank Baum]

The End

The main character, Dorothy, arrives home in Kansas. Her adventures in a strange land called Oz have made her realize there's no place like home.

Build suspense with false hope and thwarted plans...

Resolution

Dorothy defeats a wicked witch and uses her magic shoes to get home.

Introduce new characters and twists along the way.

Climax!

Dorothy thinks a wise wizard will help her get back to Kansas, but he turns out to be a fake!

The journey

On her way to find the wizard, Dorothy meets other characters who also want his help.

Beginning

Everything is dreary and flat in Kansas. Then a whirlwind whisks Dorothy away to Oz.

Not a tree nor a house broke the broad sweep of flat country that reached to the edge of the sky in all directions.

Settings

Explore your story's surroundings before you start writing. If it's a fictional place, map it out. If it's a real place, look it up or – better still – visit it in person.

Map it out

List the main places where your story takes place, then plot where they are in relation to each other.

Sandberg City, Agatha's home

Track only accessible by truck

Perilous plain

Hasn't rained for months

Elephants' migration route

Encounter with lions

Hunter's lair

Oldville, a sleepy, dusty town

Make it real

Here are some other things to consider, to make your setting sound realistic:

- seasons
- vegetation
- weather conditions
- modes of transport
- passing of time
- language spoken

Pick and choose

Don't try to describe everything about a location. Let useful details emerge as the plot advances.

The camp was completely surrounded by barbed wire.

This suggests they don't want any visitors.

Agatha weaved her way through the on-coming tide of commuters and dived into the nearest cafe.

We now know that Agatha lives in a busy city.

The road petered out and an endless, rocky plain opened out before them.

It's going to be a rough ride.

Sweat dripped from her forehead, making long streaks down her dusty face.

It's hot and dry.

Setting the scene

Think of your story as a series of scenes in a play or a film. What's the next location? Who's on stage or screen now?

Scene change

It's fine to jump from one setting to another. Just give your readers enough information so they can keep up.

A new chapter in a novel is something like a new scene in a play; and when I draw up the curtain this time, reader, you must fancy you see a room in the George Inn at Millcote...

[The beginning of chapter 11 of *Jane Eyre* by Charlotte Brontë]

Giving a place a name makes it seem more real.

Character types

Most stories revolve around a few central figures.
Here are some examples of the main ones.

Protagonist

Also known as:
the hero or heroine

Examples: Hamlet,
a superhero,
Alice (in Wonderland)

Role: the whole story revolves
around this character

Mother figure

Examples: fairy
godmothers in fairy tales,
Wendy in *Peter Pan*

Role: to provide
comfort and help for
the protagonist

Antagonist

Also known as:
the villain or baddie

Examples: the White
Witch, Dracula, the
sheriff of Nottingham

Role: to thwart
the protagonist

Love interest

Examples: Mr. Rochester
in *Jane Eyre*, Ophelia
in *Hamlet*

Role: to give the
protagonist added
purpose, support or
heartache

Sidekick

Examples: Dr. Watson
in *Sherlock Holmes*,
Robin in *Batman*

Role: to aid the
protagonist

Role model

Examples: the wizard
Merlin, the goddess
Athena

Role: to advise, guide
and maybe train the
protagonist

Find ideas for character names via the Usborne Quicklinks website.

Stock characters

The same types of minor characters crop up again and again in stories. They're known as stock characters.

Absent-minded
professor

Boy next door

Hag

Femme fatale

Mad scientist

Alien

Cat-loving
old lady

Knight on
a quest

Role tip

Try combining several characters in one, e.g. the mad scientist could also be the sidekick.

Avoiding stereotypes

It's fine to use a stock character as a starting point, but then add some original traits to make your character unique.

The cat-loving old lady
is a stereotype...

...but what if she is
covered in tattoos...

...and has an addiction
to popcorn?

Piecing it together

Complicated storylines may need careful piecing together. Here are some suggestions.

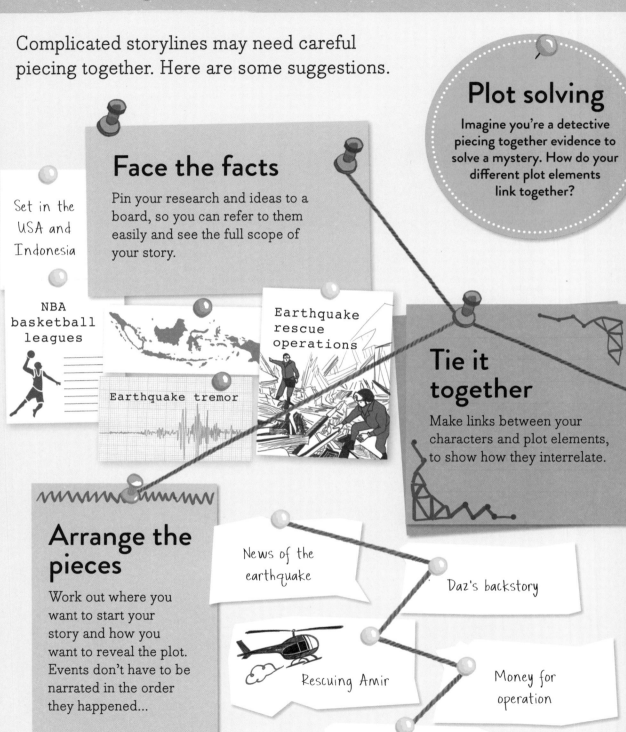

Plot solving

Imagine you're a detective piecing together evidence to solve a mystery. How do your different plot elements link together?

Set in the USA and Indonesia

NBA basketball leagues

Face the facts

Pin your research and ideas to a board, so you can refer to them easily and see the full scope of your story.

Earthquake rescue operations

Earthquake tremor

Tie it together

Make links between your characters and plot elements, to show how they interrelate.

Arrange the pieces

Work out where you want to start your story and how you want to reveal the plot. Events don't have to be narrated in the order they happened...

News of the earthquake

Daz's backstory

Rescuing Amir

Money for operation

Basketball star

Go to the next section for advice on how to get writing!

Shifting goals

As your characters face one event after another, their goals and priorities are likely to change. Make sure your storyline changes with them.

At the end

Earning money for Amir's operation was what mattered most...

DAZ'S GOALS

Before the earthquake

Being selected for the basketball team was all that mattered.

After the earthquake

Finding his cousin Amir was all that mattered.

...and earning it through playing basketball was a dream come true!

Spreadsheet

Take a leaf out of J. K. Rowling's book and draw up a spreadsheet. That's how the Harry Potter novels were planned out.

Spreadsheets help you to keep track of more than one main character.

WHEN	DAZ'S STORY	AMIR'S STORY
20th March	Daz is scouted for the Boston team.	Amir visits relatives in Indonesia.
2nd April	Daz misses his basketball trial and flies to Indonesia.	Amir is missing after an earthquake.
5th April	Daz joins the rescue mission.	Amir is rescued but needs urgent care.
10th April	Daz is called up to play in basketball final.	The basketball earnings pay for Amir's operation.

Writing stories

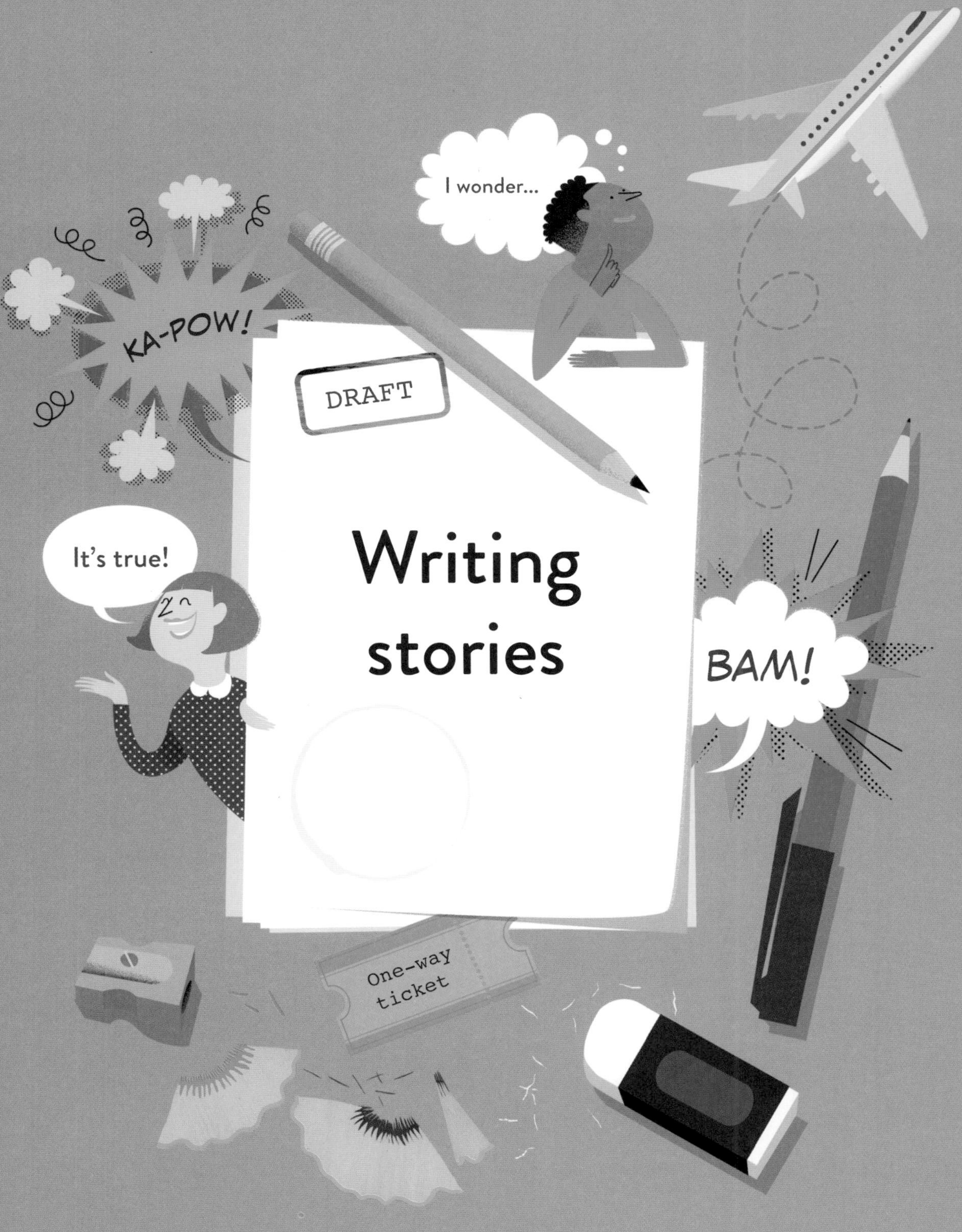

Openers

Your opening line should hook your readers and encourage them to read on. Here are some ideas on how to begin your story.

Set the scene

Open with a strong image that sets the scene for the entire story.

In a hole in the ground there lived a hobbit.

[From *The Hobbit* by J. R. R. Tolkein]

This opener draws the reader into a strange world where creatures called hobbits exist.

Establish a voice

Introduce your narrator's unique voice. How does he or she address the reader?

TRUE! – nervous – very, very dreadfully nervous I had been and am; but why will you say that I am mad?

[From "The Tell-Tale Heart" by Edgar Allan Poe]

Hint at trouble

Start with an immediate threat, challenge or suggestion of trouble.

"Where's Papa going with that axe?" said Fern to her mother as they were setting the table for breakfast.

[From *Charlotte's Web* by E. B. White]

In this children's story about a pig, the mention of an axe immediately creates a feeling of unease.

Surprise!

Catch your readers off guard with a surprising opener that raises lots of questions.

It was a bright cold day in April, and the clocks were striking thirteen.

[From *1984* by George Orwell]

Endings

Make sure you give your story a satisfying ending. Here are some different ways you could finish it.

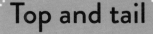

Tie things up

Tie up all the loose ends of the plot, and explain the fate of your main characters. Don't leave any unanswered questions.

The next day the prince took his bride to his father's palace, and there they lived happily ever afterward.

[From *Sleeping Beauty* by Charles Perrault]

A twist in the tale

End your story with a twist (a dramatic revelation or unexpected turn of events) to shock your readers and leave them thinking. The French short story writer Guy de Maupassant was famous for his twist endings, like this one:

"Oh, my poor Mathilde! But mine was imitation. It was worth at the very most five hundred francs! ..."

[From "The Necklace" by Guy de Maupassant]

Here, Mathilde realizes that the diamond necklace she'd borrowed, lost, and replaced at great expense, was actually fake.

Top and tail

Once you've written the ending, have a look at your opening again. It may need rewriting if your story took an unexpected route.

Leave it open

Alternatively, you could leave your ending open to interpretation and let your readers form their own conclusions.

So we beat on, boats against the current, borne back ceaselessly into the past.

[From *The Great Gatsby* by F. Scott Fitzgerald]

This line has been interpreted in lots of ways — but it suggests that there is no final ending to the story.

For some sentence starter words, see page 92.

Storytelling blocks

There are five main building blocks used in storytelling.
Most stories use a mixture of all five.

HELLLLP!

Shall we?

Let's!

Action

Function: Shows what the characters are doing and what happens next.

Effect: Makes the plot move quickly.

Warning: A story that's all action can be exhausting for the reader. Try to intersperse other blocks.

Dialogue

Function: Allows you to hear the story in the characters' own words.

Effect: Breaks up the narration and makes characters seem more real.

Warning: Each character should have a different perspective, agenda and way of talking. They can't tell the whole story.

Description

Function: Sets the scene and shows the reader what the characters are seeing, hearing, smelling, etc.

Effect: Paces the plot by breaking up the action.

Warning: You can't describe everything. Choose carefully.

Inner thoughts

Function: Lets the reader know what's going on inside the characters' heads.

Effect: Gives the characters emotional depth.

Warning: Don't expose the characters too much. Let their thoughts come out gradually.

Nobody knows, except me and the reader...

Use your words to paint a picture.

Russ was the life and soul of the party, until the fateful accident. Now he seemed to be avoiding everyone.

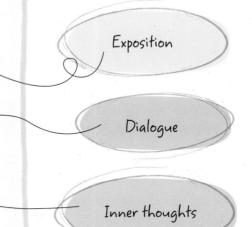

Exposition

"He's lost his sparkle," sighed Dinah. "He lost his leg!" Carrie cried.

Dialogue

Really, thought Carrie. Dinah can be so insensitive at times. Can't she think of someone else's feelings for a change?

Inner thoughts

At that moment, the double doors swung open onto the playground and Russ himself began hobbling towards them.

Action

As his hunched figure drew nearer, the girls noticed the lines of frustration and pain carved deep in his forehead.

Description

Exposition

Function: Introduces background information. Summarizes and explains the situation.

Effect: Gives an overview and context for the story.

Warning: Exposition takes you away from the drama of the story. Only use it where necessary.

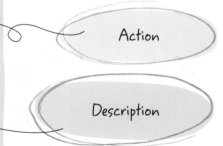

Story tip

Be flexible. An adventure story will need a different balance of blocks to a romantic novel.

Find more on story elements via the Usborne Quicklinks website.

Action

Well-written action scenes can take the reader on a nail-biting, white-knuckled rollercoaster ride.

Action starters

Kick-start the action by giving your character something to react to.

A surprise email

A chance meeting

A challenge or a threat

Short sentences

Short, punchy sentences quicken the pace. They add drama. And urgency.

Minimal dialogue

Don't give the characters too much to say or it can break the tension.

Yikes!

I feel sick...

Active verbs

Choose strong verbs that give more energy and meaning to the action.

Catapulted over the wall

Erupted into the room

Screeched to a halt

Brakes on...

Even in a high octane scene you need to put the brakes on at times. Let your readers catch their breath... before you step on the accelerator again.

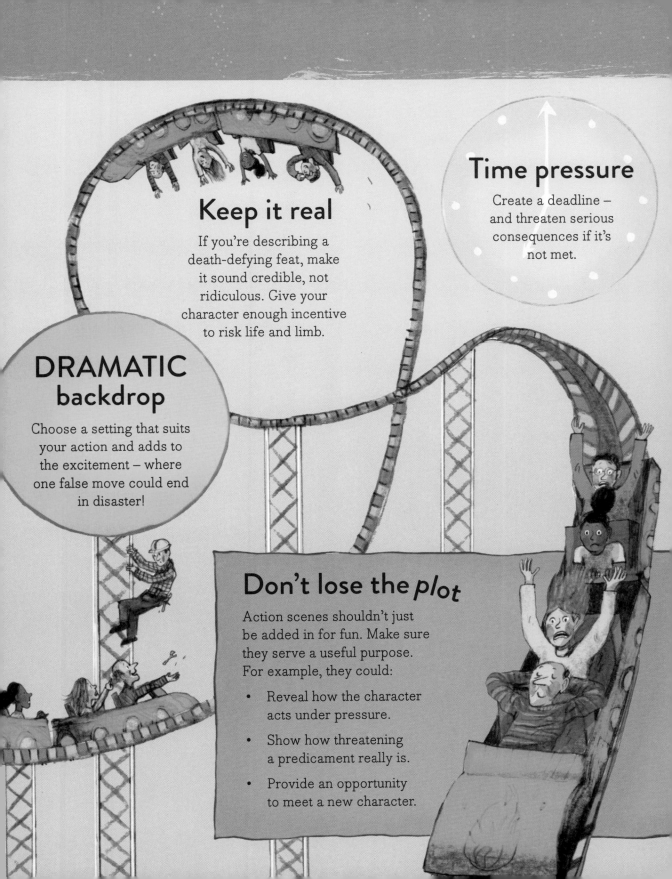

Keep it real

If you're describing a death-defying feat, make it sound credible, not ridiculous. Give your character enough incentive to risk life and limb.

Time pressure

Create a deadline – and threaten serious consequences if it's not met.

DRAMATIC backdrop

Choose a setting that suits your action and adds to the excitement – where one false move could end in disaster!

Don't lose the *plot*

Action scenes shouldn't just be added in for fun. Make sure they serve a useful purpose. For example, they could:

- Reveal how the character acts under pressure.

- Show how threatening a predicament really is.

- Provide an opportunity to meet a new character.

Dialogue

Dialogue breathes life into characters and helps the plot to progress. Try to make their words as convincing as possible.

> Hey, that's *my* tutu!

> You're just jealous of my oh-so-long legs.

Eavesdrop

Pretend you're eavesdropping on your characters. Choose a key moment in the plot and imagine what's being said.

> Try saying the words out loud. How do they sound?

Lara: Hey, that's _my_ tutu!
Rav: You're just jealous of my oh-so-long legs.

Jot it down

Don't worry about speech directions to start with. Just jot down the exchange of words, as if they were lines in a script.

Write it up

Use inverted commas (speech marks) to separate direct speech from the rest of a sentence.

Add enough direction to show who's saying what.

> Always start speech with a capital letter...

> ...apart from when a sentence is broken up.

> Characters convey meaning with their actions, as well as their words.

"Hey that's _my_ tutu," said Lara, struggling to keep herself from smiling.

"You're just jealous," Rav teased, "of my oh-so-long legs."

I said, he said, she said

It's ok to repeat the word 'said'. In fact, it's preferable to stumbling over 'apologized', 'explained', 'elaborated' and other longer words.

Even better, leave out the speech directions completely – so long as it's clear who's speaking.

Talking tip

Avoid writing whole conversations. Only include dialogue that advances the plot.

This description reveals Scrooge's true nature, not just how he's speaking.

"How now?" said Scrooge, caustic and cold as ever. "What do you want with me?"
"MUCH!" – Marley's voice, no doubt about it.
"Who are you?"
"Ask me who I was."

[From *A Christmas Carol* by Charles Dickens]

No need for 'said' – it's clear now who's talking.

Speech habits

Everyone speaks differently. Here are some speech habits you could give to your characters.

- Frequently repeating a particular phrase, e.g. "Told you so."

- An abrupt manner

- A tendency to gabble

- Stammering when nervous

- A predilection for long words

- Resorting to silence when annoyed or upset

- Always finishing other people's sentences

Writing accents

Speech can sound more authentic if you capture a person's accent in your writing. Don't overdo it though, or the words will become too hard to read.

Listen to different accents via the Usborne Quicklinks website.

"'Tisn't a city, the place I mean; leastwise 'twaddn' when I was there – 'twas a little one-eyed, blinking sort o' place."

[From *Tess of the d'Urbervilles* by Thomas Hardy]

Unusual turns of phrase add interest to a character.

Description

Descriptions enable readers to picture scenes and situations for themselves.

Here's an extract from *Little Women*, showing different examples of descriptive writing.

Sketch it out

Describe enough detail for your readers to visualize the characters and their surroundings.

Personification

Lend human traits to non-human things. It can make your descriptions more vivid.

Adjectives

Adjectives are the main describing words. Use them to describe atmosphere and emotion as well as people and places.

Analogy

Vary your descriptions by making an analogy – comparing a person or thing to someone or something else.

Little Women

As young readers like to know 'how people look', we will take this moment to give them a little sketch of the four sisters, who sat knitting away in the twilight, while the December snow fell quietly without, and the fire crackled cheerfully within. [...]

← Personification

Margaret, the eldest of the four, was sixteen, and very pretty, being plump and fair, with large eyes, plenty of soft brown hair, a sweet mouth, and white hands, of which she was rather vain.

Adjectives

Fifteen-year-old Jo was very tall, thin, and brown, and reminded one of a colt, for she never seemed to know what to do with her long limbs, which were very much in her way.

Analogy

[From *Little Women* by Louisa May Alcott]

Imagery

Use devices such as similes and metaphors to conjure up images and give readers new insights.

The moon was a ghostly galleon tossed upon cloudy seas.

[From "The Highwayman", a poem by Alfred Noyes]

Her romantic mind was like the tiny boxes, one within the other, that come from the puzzling East.

[From *Peter Pan* by J. M. Barrie]

Metaphors compare two things by saying that one is the other.

Similes use the word 'like' or 'as' to compare two things.

Paper clip moments

Some of the most memorable descriptions focus on a single, poignant detail. The crime novelist Raymond Chandler gives an excellent example in one of his letters:

...the things [the readers] remembered, that haunted them, were not for example that a man got killed, but that in the moment of his death he was trying to pick a paper clip up off the polished surface of a desk, and it kept slipping away from him, so that there was a look of strain on his face and his mouth was half open in a kind of tormented grin...

Try to home in on your own paper clip moments.

Description suggestions

- Avoid generalizations.
- Describe things from your character's point of view.
- Forget that you know what an object *is* – simply describe what it *looks like*.
- Evoke smells and sounds as well as sights.
- Use comparisons to enhance your imagery.

There's more about descriptive language on pages 64-65.

Inner thoughts

Inner thoughts are when characters speak to themselves.
Readers can 'listen in' on their thoughts, but other characters can't.

The thoughts are written like speech, except they don't need speech marks.

Use 'I' and 'me' to show you're inside the character's mind.

But what have I done with my life? thought Mrs Ramsay.

[From *To the Lighthouse* by Virginia Woolf]

Tag words such as 'thought' or 'wondered' indicate that the preceding words are inner thoughts.

Italics?

Some writers use italics for inner thoughts. Others use speech marks and many use neither. All three techniques are fine. Just choose one and stick to it.

Who's thinking?

Don't dip in and out of different characters' heads. Only write inner thoughts for the main observer in a scene. It avoids confusion.

When to use inner thoughts

- To reveal the truth about a character – his or her hopes, fears, dreams and motivations.

- To add humour or sarcasm – what a character really thinks is often very different to what is spoken out loud.

- For characters to give themselves a pep talk – tell themselves off or spur themselves on.

- To slow down the pace of a scene – give your character (and reader) time to reflect.

Exposition

Exposition is when you fill in gaps in your reader's knowledge of a story. There are many different ways to present exposition.

Through narration

Stories or chapters often start with the narrator setting the scene. This is a quick and easy way to introduce background information.

> A long time ago in a galaxy far, far away...

[The opening words for the *Star Wars* films]

> Here's an example of narration in the third person.

> I will begin the story of my adventures with a certain morning early in the month of June...

[The first line of *Kidnapped* by Robert Louis Stevenson]

> Narration can also be in the first person.

Through flashbacks

An incident triggers a character to remember and recount a previous event.

Through extracts

Reveal information about recent events through inserting emails, articles, letters, diary entries etc.

That night, Brian received an unexpected email:

From: Headmaster
To: Brian
We would like to make you head boy.

> Extracts help break up the text and vary the exposition.

Through dialogue

Let your characters do the explaining for you, by putting juicy gossip in their conversations.

> Did you hear what happened to Nancy last Friday?

Scripts

There are lots of different ways to tell a story. Try writing a script for a play, film, radio or TV show.

Script format

Scripts need to be clearly presented, so it's obvious who's doing what.

Set the scene

Break your script up into a series of scenes. Say where and when each scene is set and list which characters are in the scene.

Who's speaking?

Write the character's name on the left each time he or she speaks, followed by a colon.

Stage directions

Stage directions are instructions to the actors and director. They can be written in brackets or as separate lines of text.

Enter and exit

Make it clear if someone arrives or leaves a scene by using the words 'enter' and 'exit'.

Write the names of the characters in capitals so they stand out.

SCENE 21

Internal hall at Bytheways, next morning. ELIZABETH enters from the sitting room. VICKY rushes down the stairs with the magazine she was reading last night. She holds up the article in one hand and a riding whip in the other.

VICKY: Mummie, can you buy me a bigger whip than this, please. I am going to be a female lion tamer.

ELIZABETH: No.

VICKY: You said girls can do anything boys can do.
                   (beat)
                   I will also need a lion.

ELIZABETH raises a sardonic sort of eyebrow. After a moment, VICKY exits by flouncing through into the sitting room.

[From *Diary of a Provincial Lady*, adapted for stage by Robert Hudson]

A 'beat' is the pause a character takes to separate his or her thoughts.

Turn to page 51 to see how scripts are used to write comics.

48

Which script?

Decide whether you're writing for stage, screen or radio. Each medium needs a different approach.

Play scripts

Plays are restricted by what you can show on stage. Car chases and huge crowd scenes are best avoided, or described after the event.

I've just fought my way through a screaming mob!

Film and TV scripts

For screenplays, the action can jump around a lot more. Think of where the camera is pointing in each scene and include a description of what's in view.

Lights... Camera... Action!

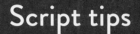

Radio scripts

Writing for radio is all about the sound, since the listener can't see anything. Include sound effects in brackets.

(Knock at the door)

(Sound of breaking glass)

Script tips

The characters

- Make them unique.
- Make them vulnerable.
- Give each character something they want or need, to create purpose.
- Adapt speech to reflect a character's mood and who he or she is talking to.

The plot

- Find a compelling journey for the character and audience to go on.
- Begin the drama with a significant moment.
- Add highs and lows, dead ends and moments when everything becomes clear.
- Show that actions have consequences.

Dialogue

- All dialogue should be there for a reason.
- Make each voice distinct and identifiable.
- Include silences too, for the things not said.
- What people say and what they really mean isn't always the same thing.

Comics

Comic strips and graphic novels use illustrated scenes and speech bubbles to tell stories.

Panels

Comics are made up of boxes called panels. You usually read them from left to right. They can vary in size, to suit each scene.

Speech bubbles

Speech is written in speech bubbles. These are mostly oval shapes, with a tail pointing at the speaker.

Find more comic writing ideas via the Usborne Quicklinks website.

Write a script

Comics are often written as scripts before they're illustrated. For each panel, describe the scene, then write out the caption and dialogue text.

Don't panic

You don't have to be a great artist to create good comics. You just need strong ideas... and a few stick figures!

Write the names in capitals of the main characters in the panel.

List the text entries for each panel in the order people should read them.

Panel 1

CINDERELLA makes a grand, late entrance to the ball. Show the PRINCE mesmerized and the STEPSISTERS fuming in the foreground.

1. CAPTION: All eyes were on the dazzling princess.
2. STEPSISTER A: Look at that dress!
3. STEPSISTER B: I've seen curtains with more style.

There's more about script writing on pages 48-49.

Doodle then draw

Try rough sketches for your characters and settings, before you tackle the main panel pictures.

Make sure you design in enough space for your speech bubbles.

Titles

A good title is attention-grabbing and makes people want to read your story. Here are some ways to come up with the perfect title.

Title tip

It's a good idea to wait until you've finished writing your story before you start choosing a title.

Find a theme

You might find a title in your story itself – look for a key theme, a central character, or a phrase that sums up the story.

On the Road to West Egg
Trimalchio in West Egg
The High-Bouncing Lover
Gold-Hatted Gatsby
Under the Red, White and Blue
Among Ash-Heaps and Millionaires

This is a list of titles F. Scott Fitzgerald came up with for his novel *The Great Gatsby*.

This is a reference to the American flag. America is a central theme of the novel.

Tempt your readers

Make your title sound catchy and intriguing, so your readers will want to tell their friends about it.

The Two Towers

Of Mice and Men

Wuthering Heights

JURASSIC PARK

Heart of Darkness

The Boy Who Sailed The Ocean In An Armchair

Try using alliteration (words with repeated consonant sounds).

Settings and place names can make emotive titles.

These titles paint powerful visual descriptions.

Borrow from others

Lift words and phrases from an existing work, such as a poem, book or song.

> I have forgot much, Cynara! gone with the wind,
> Flung roses, roses riotously with the throng…
>
> [From "Non sum qualis eram bonae sub regno Cynarae" by Ernest Dowson]

This poem about lost love inspired Margaret Mitchell's famous novel, *Gone with the Wind*.

Covers

A cover should entice people to pick your book off the shelf. Think of the cover as an advertisement that's selling a product (your story).

Find out how to use words to sell a product on pages 72-73.

Title

Make sure your title is clear and well incorporated into the design.

Images

Try using simple images that appeal to people's emotions.

Colours

Use a colour scheme that captures the overall tone of your story.

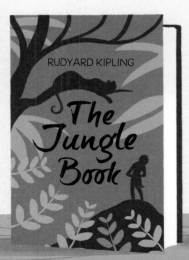

RUDYARD KIPLING

The Jungle Book

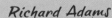

Richard Adams

Watership Down

FRANKENSTEIN

MARY SHELLEY

claws that catch
Bandersnatch

beautiful
pea-green
boat

Poetry
and song

a host of
golden daffodils

What is a poem?

Poems use imaginative language to express ideas and emotions. There are many different types of poems.

Here are a few descriptions of poems by poets.

Poetry is like a bird, it ignores all frontiers.

[Yevgeny Yevtushenko]

...imaginary gardens with real toads in them.

[Marianne Moore]

A poem makes you laugh, cry, prickle, be silent, makes your toe nails twinkle...

[Dylan Thomas]

Making music

In ancient times, poems were set to music. Sound is still an important part of poetry – imagine your poem as a song in which the words make music.

I celebrate myself, and sing myself,
And what I assume you shall assume,
For every atom belonging to me as good belongs to you.

I loafe and invite my soul,
I lean and loafe at my ease observing a spear of summer grass.

[From "Song of Myself" by Walt Whitman]

A group of lines is called a 'stanza'.

There are lots more examples of lyric poems on pages 58-65.

Groups of poetry

Poetry can be divided into three main groups – lyric, narrative or dramatic.

Lyric

A lyric poem is a way to express your personal feelings and state of mind.

'Hope' is the thing with feathers
That perches in the soul,
And sings the tune without the words,
And never stops at all.

[From "'Hope' is the thing with feathers" by Emily Dickinson]

Narrative

Tell a story with a plot, characters and a setting if you're writing a narrative poem.

Once upon a midnight dreary, while I pondered, weak and weary,
Over many a quaint and curious volume of forgotten lore—
While I nodded, nearly napping, suddenly there came a tapping,
As of some one gently rapping, rapping at my chamber door...

[From "The Raven" by Edgar Allan Poe]

Dramatic

A dramatic poem is a narrative poem that's intended to be spoken or sung on stage.

Two households, both alike in dignity,
In fair Verona, where we lay our scene,
From ancient grudge break to new mutiny,
Where civil blood makes civil hands unclean.

[From *Romeo and Juliet* by William Shakespeare]

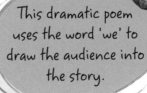

This dramatic poem uses the word 'we' to draw the audience into the story.

Rhyme and metre

When you're writing a poem, it helps to say it out loud.
All poems have a rhythm and music of their own.

Rhyme

You can use rhyme – words that share
the same sound – to tie your lines
together. Here are two examples:

This poem uses assonance
– rhyming words with
repeated vowel sounds.

The Owl and the Pussy-cat went to sea
In a beautiful pea green boat,
They took some honey, and plenty of money,
Wrapped up in a five pound note.

[From *The Book of Nonsense* by Edward Lear]

Listen for alliteration
here – words with repeated
consonant sounds.

She sells seashells on the seashore;
The shells that she sells are seashells I'm sure.
So if she sells seashells on the seashore,
I'm sure that the shells are seashore shells.

["She Sells Seashells" by Anon.]

Rhyme schemes

When the rhyming lines in a poem make a pattern,
this is called a rhyme scheme. Try creating your own
rhyme scheme – it will help your poem flow.

I wandered lonely as a cloud   A
That floats on high o'er vales and hills,   B
When all at once I saw a crowd,   A
A host, of golden daffodils;   B
Beside the lake, beneath the trees,   C
Fluttering and dancing in the breeze. C

[From "Daffodils" by William Wordsworth]

These letters show
the rhyme scheme.
In this case, it's
ABABCC.

Metre

Most poems have their own rhythm, or 'metre'. When you read a poem aloud, listen out for the hard and soft sounds – or stressed and unstressed syllables – in each line. These set the metre.

Say the nursery rhyme below out loud, and listen to the different sounds the words make:

The nursery rhyme's metre is written out below in sounds. 'DUM' is a stress, and 'da' is an unstressed syllable.

JACK and JILL went UP the HILL

to FETCH a PAIL of WA-ter.

JACK fell DOWN and BROKE his CROWN,

and JILL came TUMbling AFT-er.

["Jack and Jill", a traditional nursery rhyme]

DUM da DUM da DUM da DUM

da DUM da DUM da DUM da

DUM da DUM da DUM da DUM

da DUM da DUM da DUM da

 Watch videos about metre including iambic pentameter via the Usborne Quicklinks website.

An unstressed syllable followed by a stressed syllable is called an iamb.

Five iambs

The most common type of metre in English poetry is 'iambic pentameter', which contains five iambs in a line. Here's an example, with the sounds written out underneath:

Shall I compare thee to a summer's day?

da DUM da DUM da DUM da DUM da DUM

❶　　❷　　❸　　❹　　❺

[From "Sonnet 18" by William Shakespeare]

The 'da DUM' of an iamb is often compared to a human heartbeat.

Most of Shakespeare's sonnets (14-line poems) are written in iambic pentameter.

Poetic forms

A poem's structure – or the way in which its words are organized – is known as its form. Here are some different forms of poetry.

Free verse

Free verse is a poem without a regular rhyme scheme or metre. It usually follows the natural pattern of speech.

> Beat! beat! drums! – blow! bugles! blow!
> Through the windows – through doors – burst like a ruthless force,
> Into the solemn church, and scatter the congregation,
> Into the school where the scholar is studying...
>
> [From "Beat! Beat! Drums!" by Walt Whitman]

Instead of using a rhyme scheme, try repeating words for emphasis.

Mix long and short lines together.

Haiku

Haiku is a very short form of poem invented in Japan. Its first line has five syllables, the second has seven, and the third has five.

Most haiku refer to a specific season. Here, frogs suggest the rainy season in Japan.

1 2 3 4 5
An old silent pond...
1 2 3 4 5 6 7
A frog jumps into the pond,
1 2 3 4 5
splash! Silence again.

[By Matsuo Bashō]

Concrete poem

A concrete poem is arranged in a shape on the page. The shape usually matches the subject of the poem. Here's an example:

> Draw an outline of your shape first, then fill it with words.

> You could vary the size of your words and letters, like this.

This poem is based on a clever pun – it's a tale about a tail, written in the shape of a mouse's tail.

"Fury said to
a mouse, That
he met in the
house, 'Let
us both go
to law: I
will pros-
ecute *you*.
- Come, I'll
take no
denial; We
must have
the trial: For
really this
morning
I've noth-
ing to
do.' Said
the mouse
to the cur,
'Such a
trial, dear
sir, With
no jury
or judge
would
be wast-
ing our
breath.'
'I'll be
judge,
I'll be
jury,'
said
cun-
ning
old
Fury:
'I'll
try the
whole
cause,
and
con-
demn
you to
death.

[Extract from *Alice's Adventures in Wonderland* by Lewis Carroll]

Break the rules

Writing poetry is about being creative with words, so you don't have to stick to grammar rules.

More poetic forms

Sonnet: A 14-line poem with ten syllables in each line.

Ode: A poem that addresses a person or thing.

Limerick: A funny five-line poem with a strong beat.

Epic: A long narrative poem about a hero's adventures.

Listen to haiku and read different forms of poetry via the Usborne Quicklinks website.

Song lyrics

The words that make up a song are called lyrics. You can write your lyrics before, after or at the same time as composing the music.

There are many different kinds of songs. Here are a few examples.

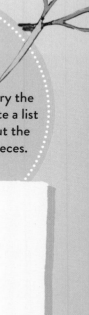

Cut-up writing

If you're stuck for lyric ideas, try the 'cut-up writing' technique. Write a list of phrases onto paper, then cut the paper up and rearrange the pieces.

Ballads

A ballad is a song (or a poem) that tells a story. Try breaking your lyrics into two or more verses and a repeated chorus, like the ballad on the right.

Verse

Put the main body of your lyrics in the verse. Each verse has the same melody, but different lyrics.

Chorus

The song's central theme or message goes in the chorus or refrain.

In Dublin's fair city,
Where the girls are so pretty,
I first set my eyes on sweet Molly Malone,
As she wheeled her wheel-barrow,
Through streets broad and narrow,
Crying, "Cockles and mussels, alive, alive, o!"

Alive, alive o, alive, alive o,
Crying "Cockles and mussels, alive, alive o!"

She was a fishmonger,
But sure 'twas no wonder,
For so were her father and mother before,
And they each wheeled their barrow,
Through streets broad and narrow,
Crying, "Cockles and mussels, alive, alive, o!"

Alive, alive o, alive, alive o,
Crying "Cockles and mussels, alive, alive o!"

["Cockles and Mussels"
by Anon.]

This Irish ballad tells the story of a fishmonger from Dublin. It uses lots of repetition, which makes the words easy to remember.

Listen to the songs mentioned in this book via the Usborne Quicklinks website.

Western songs

During the 19th century, the people who settled in western America sang songs celebrating working life and the great outdoors.

Oh give me a home where the buffalo roam,
Where the deer and the antelope play,
Where seldom is heard a discouraging word,
And the skies are not cloudy all day.

Home, home on the range,
Where the deer and the antelope play,
Where seldom is heard a discouraging word,
And the skies are not cloudy all day.

["Home on the Range" by Anon.]

Use hyperbole (exaggeration) to create an idealized view.

Musicals

Musicals are plays that include a mixture of spoken dialogue and songs. Try writing lyrics that show the audience what your characters are thinking or feeling.

Capitalize your song lyrics to set them apart from the spoken dialogue.

PENNY
BOXER AND I WILL WIN THE GRAND NATIONAL.
BOXER
SHE IS IRRATIONAL: YOU GET USED TO IT.
PENNY
BOXER WILL WIN A SHINY RED APPLE,
I'LL WIN A BIG ROSETTE.
BOXER AND I WILL BE THE OUTSIDERS,
ALL OTHER RIDERS WILL HAVE BETTER ODDS.
NO ONE WILL THINK WE'RE GOING TO WIN IT.
BOXER
NO ONE, INCLUDING ME.

[From *Farm!* by Susannah Pearse and Robert Hudson]

Write the names of the characters who are singing in bold.

Poetic language

Poets and songwriters use words to create different effects, or convey several meanings at once. Here are some examples for you to try.

Onomatopoeia

Add sound effects using onomatopoeia – words that sound like their meanings.

There was a rustling that seemed like a bustling
Of merry crowds justling at pitching and hustling,
Small feet were pattering, wooden shoes clattering,
Little hands clapping and little tongues chattering,
And, like fowls in a farm-yard when barley is scattering,
Out came the children running.

[From "The Pied Piper of Hamelin" by Robert Browning]

These onomatopoeic words convey a feeling of excitement and anticipation.

Cacophony

Create the feeling of disorder by using a mixture of harsh sounding, discordant words.

Beware the Jabberwock, my son!
The jaws that bite, the claws that catch!

[From "Jabberwocky" in *Through the Looking Glass and What Alice Found There* by Lewis Carroll]

Use words with hard-sounding consonants, such as 'j', 'b' and 'cl'.

Euphony

Mix words with harmonious, pleasing sounds to create a soothing effect.

To bend with apples the moss'd cottage-trees,
And fill all fruit with ripeness to the core;
To swell the gourd, and plump the hazel shells...

[From "Ode to Autumn" by John Keats]

Try soft-sounding vowels and consonants such as 'f', 'm', 'sw' and 'ou'.

Hyperbole

Emphasize a feeling using exaggeration, also known as hyperbole (say hi-PER-bo-lee).

I'll love you, dear, I'll love you
Till China and Africa meet,
And the river jumps over the mountain
And the salmon sing in the street...

[From "As I Walked Out One Evening" by W. H. Auden]

You can use hyperbole to create comic effects, like this.

Symbolism

Use an object to represent an idea or emotion that's difficult to describe in words – such as love, death, hope or friendship.

O Rose thou art sick.
The invisible worm,
That flies in the night
In the howling storm:

Has found out thy bed
Of crimson joy:
And his dark secret love
Does thy life destroy.

["The Sick Rose" by William Blake]

Here, the rose is a symbol of love, while the worm is a symbol of death and decay.

Writing tips

- Think visually and pick words that evoke a strong image.

- Avoid clichés (these are overused phrases, such as 'busy as a bee' or 'fresh as a daisy').

- Use language that your reader will understand.

- Don't be afraid to write honestly and expressively.

- Make every word count.

65

Non-fiction

Awesome Animal Facts

My blog

8th March

Dear Diary,
You won't believe what
happened to me today.
I'm still pinching myself
to check it was real!

Mystery planet

The Daily News

SHIPWRECKED!

Reports

Reports state the facts of a topic as clearly and concisely as possible.

Layout

A neat, organized layout makes a report much easier to read.

Title

Give your report a main title that's short and to the point.

Introduction

In the first paragraph set out what your report is about.

Categories

Divide your information into categories and write about each one under a suitable subheading.

Bullet points

It can be helpful to break up information using bullet points. Introduce points with a sentence ending in a colon (:).

The Eating Habits of Cats

Cats are carnivores. They need a meat-based diet to stay fit and healthy. Wild cats hunt for their food, while domestic cats rely on their owners to make the right decisions.

Use capital letters in the title, except for small joining words, e.g. 'of'.

Hunting

Cats are natural hunters, pouncing on rodents and small birds. Although pet cats don't need to hunt for their food, it remains a strong habit.

Manufactured food

There are three main types of cat food available for sale in supermarkets:

- Wet food in cans
- Dry food in bags
- Semi-moist food in pouches

Only use full-stops if the bullet point text is a full sentence.

You could use a mind map to plan your report – see pages 20-21.

Warning

Don't start writing a report until you've researched the topic and have all the information at your fingertips.

Writing tips

- Only include relevant information.

- Use formal language, nothing too chatty.

- Write in the third person (not 'I' or 'you').

- Write in the present tense, unless the report is historical.

- Back up explanations with facts and figures.

- Add comments and questions to keep the reader engaged.

It would be interesting to see which cat food cats would buy.

Could a domestic cat survive in the wild?

Fact not opinion

Reports should not be influenced by the writer's personal opinion. Don't say what you think or believe, but what you know from your research to be true.

If you include other people's opinions, make sure you credit them and keep their ideas separate to the main factual content.

According to Dr. Squeak, fitting a little bell to a cat's collar can greatly reduce the number of mouse fatalities.

A comment gives the reader something to think about.

Questions can be answered in the report or left open ended.

Using images

Reports can benefit from diagrams, photos or illustrations, to help get across an idea or simply to liven up the page.

Use captions and labels to make the most of your images and to give across more information.

Happy

Tail up and curled

Worried

Head slightly lowered

Angry

Hair raised and back arched

Blogs

A blog (short for 'web log') is an online journal that is regularly updated. It's written in a chatty, informal style.

Stay safe online

Before you start your blog, please read our internet safety tips at the Usborne Quicklinks website.

Blog name

Give your blog a catchy name that's easy to remember.

Bio

Introduce yourself to your readers in the 'bio' section. (Never use your full name or include details of where you live or go to school.)

Posts

Each new entry is called a 'post'. Choose a headline and a topic for each post.

Talk to your readers as you would talk to a friend.

Photos

Photos will grab your reader's attention. Use your own, or take them from a free website.

Lists keep the reader interested.

Amy goes abroad

About me

Hello! My name's Amy and I love to travel. Follow my blog as I share my stories, photos and travel tips.

Amy goes abroad

Sun, sea and sand

2 hours ago

I was super excited when we arrived at the hotel. Paradise! Nothing but blue skies and golden sand as far as the eyes could see...

Amy goes abroad

Top travel destinations

1 week ago

Paris is my top destination for a city break. My must-see sights include:

- The Eiffel Tower
- Montmartre
- The Musée d'Orsay

Find a focus

For more ideas on how to find a focus for your blog, see pages 10-13.

When you're picking a theme for your blog, choose something that fascinates you, so you'll have plenty to write about. Try to stick to a single theme to give your blog a strong identity.

 My weekly baking challenge

 **XTREME SPORTS**

 **The weird world of animals**

 Street style fashion

Writing tips

- Write in the first person ('I').

- Address your readers directly with 'you'.

- Break up each post into smaller chunks and add subheadings.

- Don't get too caught up in facts and figures – your readers want to know what *you* think.

- Speak your post out loud to check that it sounds like you.

Listen to your readers

Try to respond to any comments and questions from your readers. Show them that you're listening – that way, they'll want to visit your blog again. (You can control which comments are visible on your blog – and if you receive any rude or negative comments, ignore them.)

> Paris looks amazing – I can't wait to go! What was the food like?
>
> *Ellie*

Find more blogging tips via the Usborne Quicklinks website.

> Hi Ellie! The food was delicious. I ate sooo much cheese. Try the camembert – it's yummy!
>
> *Amy goes abroad*

Persuasive writing

The aim of persuasive writing is to convince your reader to do something or agree with your point of view.

When to use

Persuasive writing is very useful for posters, advertisements, speeches, magazine articles and letters.

Selling a product

Product packaging and other types of advertisements try to convince people that a product is worth buying. Here's a cereal box as an example.

Brand name

This usually suggests something positive about the product that's being sold.

Slogan

A short, memorable phrase that sums up the product's appeal.

Body copy

This is the written part of the advertisement, which focuses on the product's selling points.

Morning Star Cereals

HONEY HOOPS

PUT A LITTLE BUZZ INTO YOUR BREAKFAST BOWL!

TRY OUR DELICIOUS WHOLEWHEAT HOOPS!

MADE WITH 100% NATURAL HONEY

Warning

Avoid making any claims about your product that aren't supported by facts.

Show why your product is better than anyone else's.

A campaign letter

A campaign letter tries to influence people and inspire change. Try writing a letter to someone in authority about something you'd like to change.

Introduction

Present the issue you want to address, as well as a solution.

Evidence

Give at least three pieces of evidence that support your argument.

Show you've considered different points of view.

Conclusion

Summarize the main points, and suggest how the change can be made.

End your letter formally.

Dear teachers,

I believe school uniforms are outdated. I propose that the students of Summerdale High should be allowed to wear clothes of their choice.

Although uniforms look smart, they are expensive. This creates financial worries for many families.

Use language that appeals to your readers' emotions.

Statistics also show that school uniforms make students easy targets for bullies from different schools.

School uniforms are supposed to stop students being distracted by fashion trends, but they also take away our freedom of self-expression.

Include facts to support your argument.

Although I agree that uniforms look smart and reduce the pressure to wear fashionable brands, I believe it's crucial that students are able to express their individuality. Please act now and change the school rules.

Yours sincerely,
Jacob Davis

Histories

Histories are the stories of real-life people, places and events. These include biographies, autobiographies, diaries and other true stories.

Biography

This is a detailed account of a person's life, written by someone else.

> Use historical details to set the scene.

> Put direct quotations into quotation marks.

As the war dragged on, things seemed to be getting worse. News reports on the radio told of battles being fought in Africa, Russia, Italy...

"The whole world is at war," Anne wrote in her diary. "And the end is nowhere in sight."

[From *Anne Frank* by Susanna Davidson. Anne Frank was a Jewish girl who lived during the Second World War.]

My life

If you write a biography about yourself for others to read, it's called an autobiography.

Diary

This is a private account of someone's personal experiences, written in the form of entries.

> Even the smallest details can be vividly described.

> Write in the first person (I or me).

Sunday, 2 September 1666
The poor pigeons, I perceive, were loth to leave their houses, but hovered about the windows and balconys till they were, some of them burned, their wings, and fell down.

Tuesday, 4 September 1666
And in the evening, Sir W. Pen and I did dig another [hole], and put our wine in it; and I my Parmazan cheese, as well as my wine and some other things.

[From *The Diary of Samuel Pepys*. Pepys lived through the Great Fire of London of 1666. There were no standardized rules for spelling or grammar during this time.]

There are more ideas about writing descriptions on pages 44-45.

Changing a story

Histories are driven by real characters and events, but you can still be creative with the way you reveal the facts.

- Describe how things looked, sounded, smelled or felt.

- Develop your characters through action, dialogue and detailed descriptions.

- Create a strong plot line with a beginning, a middle and an end.

Find more non-fiction writing tips via Usborne Quicklinks.

Far above the Earth, satellites glide through space. Some record weather and data, others receive telephone signals.

But a few are on more secret missions. Armed with incredibly powerful cameras, spy satellites photograph enemy warships and army camps, beaming the images to secret agents below.

[From *The Story of Spying* by Rob Lloyd Jones – a non-fiction book about the history of espionage.]

Begin your story with a strong opening image.

Use dramatic, attention-grabbing words.

Research

It's important to research your topic thoroughly before you begin to write. Here are some ideas about where to begin:

- Read letters and diaries.

- Trawl through old newspapers in your local library.

- Examine photographs.

- Interview people (including friends, family, and witnesses).

- Visit relevant locations.

Warning

Avoid inventing facts or exaggerating details.

Photographs of WW2

The Andy Warhol Diaries

A History of London

Rules
and
word
lists

Editing

Editing is when you polish off your writing by correcting errors and making any last improvements.

Things to look for

Repetition

Have you explained the same thing twice without realizing it?

Have you over-used the same word when a similar word would be just as good?

It's easy to repeat the the same word and not spot the mistake.

What's wrong here?

Omissions

Are there any gaps in your plot or explanations?

Have you forgotten to introduce a character?

Are there any words

missing?

Waffle

Have you used ten words when you could have used five?

Do all the words you've chosen serve a purpose?

bla dee bla

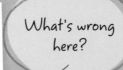

Spelling mistakes

Are there any misspellings?

If you've used a spell checker, has the wrong word slipped through?

Have you checked you've written the word you mean, not one that *sounds* the same?

Words that sound the same are called homophones.

Bad grammar

Are your sentences clear and easy to read?

Should that comma really be a full-stop?

Do your verbs match their subjects?

here or hear

your or you're

there, their or they're

bear or bare

The jury ~~have~~ has decided he's guilty.

There's only one jury, even though it's made up of lots of people.

There's some good grammar advice on pages 80-81.

How to check your writing

Print it out

If you've been using a computer, it's easier to check a print-out than to spot mistakes on a screen.

Read it slowly

Check each word carefully. Start at the end and work back if that helps.

Read it aloud

Mistakes and weak points can stand out more when you speak the words and hear them.

Wait a few days

Come back to your writing after a break and look at it again with fresh eyes.

Get a second opinion

Even the best authors get other people to check their work and suggest improvements.

Useful tools

Dictionary

For checking spellings and meanings

Thesaurus

For looking up words with similar meanings

Find an online dictionary and thesaurus via the Usborne Quicklinks website.

A spell checker

An easy way to check for misspellings on a computer

A printer

To print out a copy

A red pen!

Or green, or purple – to mark up your text clearly

Warning

Always keep a back-up copy of any writing you've done electronically. It's very easy to delete a file by mistake!

Grammar

Grammar and punctuation are the nuts and bolts of writing. They build your words into sentences.

Parts of speech

When we speak or write, we use eight different parts of speech. Knowing the function of each part helps you to understand how words fit together.

The word GRAMMAR comes from an ancient Greek phrase meaning ART OF LETTERS.

Noun
Names a person, place or thing.

lion, beach, tree, Bob

Pronoun
Is used in place of a noun.

I, me, him, she, you

Verb
Shows action or a state of being.

run, think, sit

Adjective
Describes a noun or a pronoun.

beautiful, tedious

A, **an** and **the** are special adjectives, called articles.

Preposition
Shows the relationship of a noun or a pronoun to another word.

in, on, by, with, for, from

Adverb
Describes a verb, an adjective, another adverb or sometimes a whole sentence.

quickly, very, coincidentally

Conjunction
Connects words, or groups of words.

and, but, so, because

Interjection
Expresses strong feeling or emotion.

Wow!

Example

Interjection   Adjective   Verb   Conjunction   Pronoun

Yikes! The hungry lion ran after the deer and quickly ate it.

Article   Noun   Preposition   Adverb

Building a sentence

A sentence is a group of words that makes sense on its own. It should always have a verb and a subject. The subject is the person or thing doing the verb.

Verb

Subject → Paula likes judo.

Sentences begin with a capital letter and end with a full stop, question mark or exclamation mark.

Matching subject to verb

It's important to use the right form of a verb so that it matches the subject.

Paula and Tim like tennis.

No 's' on the end of the verb when there's more than one person doing the action.

He is late and we are early.

'Is' and 'are' are different forms of the verb 'to be'.

Tenses

Tenses are the way we use verbs to indicate time. Decide whether you're writing in the past, present or future tense, and be consistent.

Past → Charlie woofed. He was dreaming of pheasants.

Present → Charlie woofs. He is dreaming of pheasants.

Future → Charlie will woof. He will be dreaming of pheasants.

Common mistakes

Here are some words people often get wrong...

I should have known.

Never 'should of'

Tea has that effect on me.
Tea affects my brain.

Effect is the noun, affect is the verb.

He brought neither an umbrella, nor a coat.

'Nor' follows 'neither', 'or' follows 'either'.

The bouquet of flowers looks stunning.

Not 'look' because 'bouquet' is the subject and there's only one.

How to check

- Look up a query in a grammar reference book.

- Download a grammar app.

- Get help with grammar via the Usborne Quicklinks website.

81

Punctuation

Punctuation is the use of special marks to signal how to read a sentence. It makes your writing easier to understand.

Comma

Function: shows the reader where to make a slight break in a sentence.

Examples:

- In lists
  red, white and blue

- In direct speech
  "Yes please," she said.

- To separate two parts of a sentence
  Although we were late, we still made the train.

- To mark off additional parts of a sentence
  My cousin, Barry, is twenty.

Full stop

Function: marks a stronger break than a comma.

Examples:

- At the end of a sentence
  Sheep like grass.

- In some abbreviations
  e.g. etc. a.m.

- In web addresses
  www.usborne.com

Semicolon

Function: stronger than a comma but not as final as a full stop.

Examples:

- In a complex list
  The winners are Joe from Paris, France; Diane from Poole, England; and Matt from Ottawa, Canada.

- Instead of a full stop
  The sky darkened; it started to rain.

Colon

Function: introduces the list, phrase or quotation that follows.

Examples:

- List
  The price includes the following: flights, car hire and accommodation.

- Phrase
  I had only one aim: to find my father.

- Quotation
  The sign read: Beware bulls.

You can also use a dash to mark a break in a sentence – like this!

Hyphen

Function: links words and parts of words.

Examples:

- In words made up of several words
  son-in-law

- To join prefixes to other words
  a mid-season match

- To show word breaks
  Freya noticed that her dog was suffering from the heat.

Shorter than a dash

Brackets

Function: separates off words that aren't essential to the sentence.

Example:

He asked Louise (his sister) for a loan.

Apostrophe

Function: either shows possession or shows letters have been taken out in a contraction.

Examples:

- Possession
  Rosa's coat, the trees' leaves

- Contraction
  you're (you are), can't (cannot)

Inverted commas

Function: marks the beginning and end of speech or a quotation. Also indicates ironic use of a word or phrase.

Can be single or double, ' or "

Examples:

- Speech
  "Yes please," he said. "I'd love to."

- Quotation
  They called it 'the final frontier'.

- Irony
  My 'reward' was to empty the bins.

Question mark

Function: marks the end of a question.

Example:

Would life ever be the same again?

Exclamation mark

Function: indicates something spoken loudly, or something amusing.

Examples:

- Shouting
  "Come here!" he cried.

- Something amusing
  She put the butter in the dishwasher!

Spy words

84

Useful research

Things to read
- Spy thrillers
- Books about the World Wars and the Cold War
- Examples of codes

Places to visit
- Museums
- Local archives
- Historic sites

Famous spies
- Mati Hari
- The Rosenbergs
- The Cambridge Five
- Giacomo Casanova

Mole
Phone hacking
Secret service
MI6
Snoop
Tap
Wire
Infiltrate
Black ops
Case operator
Cipher
Codebreaking
Compromise
Spook
Surveillance
Collaborator

Top secret
Clandestine
Agent
Double agent
Bugged
CIA
Intelligence
Covert
Decoy
Handler
Target
Cover
Safehouse
Sleeper
Asset
Brush pass
Dead drop
FBI
Traffic analysis

Planning tip

Plan out your storyline in three different acts:

1. Set-up

2. Confrontation

3. Consequences

Detective words

Mob
Gangster
Psychology
Profile
Subterfuge
Alias

Undercover
Examine
Determine
Evidence
Crime
Fingerprints
Missing
Motive
Clue
Lead
Constable
Serial killer

Crime scene
Proof
Murderer
Coincidence
Suspicious
Alibi
Breakthrough
Interrogate
Mystery
Perpetrator
Victim
Witness
Suspect
Foil
Robbery
Accomplice
Bait
Hunch

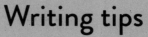

Writing tips

Use short sentences to increase suspense.

Drop hints but don't give away too much.

Include one or two red herrings.

Useful research

Things to read

- Crime novels
- News reports
- Biographies of real criminals
- Historical accounts of famous crimes

Things to visit

- Law courts
- The setting for your crime (could be anywhere)
- Police stations
- Baker Street in London (home to the fictional private detective Sherlock Holmes)

Adventure words

Sources of inspiration

Classic stories

- *Around the World in Eighty Days*
- *Treasure Island*
- *Robinson Crusoe*
- *The Three Musketeers*
- *Journey to the Centre of the Earth*
- *The Seven Voyages of Sinbad the Sailor*

Thrilling
Blood-curdling
Impenetrable
Neverending
Daring
Abyss
Supersonic
Apprehension
Stomach-turning
Brave
Fearless
Marooned

Escape
Kidnapped
Arrested
Imprison
Near miss
Close shave
Accidental
Hostage
Frostbite
Sunburn

Dreams

Some fabulous adventures can happen in your dreams. Keep a pen and paper by your bed to jot them down before you forget them.

Character tip

Create an interesting hero. The adventure will depend greatly on his or her strength of character and determination.

Famous explorers

- Christopher Columbus
- Hernán Cortés
- Sir Francis Drake
- Neil Armstrong
- Roald Amundsen
- Captain James Cook

Travel words

Departure
Itinerary
Quayside
Anticipation
Seasickness
Train station
Platform
Commute
Passport
Vacation
Exotic
Baggage
Transfer
Cruise
Culture shock
Breakdown
Invigorating
Expedition
Overwhelming
Lost in translation
Long-haul flights
Back of beyond
Destination
Unnavigable

Bewildering
Marvel
Intrepid
Delay
Disorientated
Journey

Keep a diary
Write daily accounts of your own travels, to capture the sights and smells while they're fresh in your mind.

Useful research

Books
- Travel guides
- Maps and atlases
- Travelogues (stories written by authors about their own travels)

Blogs
Read about other people's travels; their amusing anecdotes, disasters, recommendations and warnings.

Documentaries
Learn about other countries – their cultures, climate and geography – by watching travel documentaries.

Romance words

Sources of inspiration

Romantic poets

- William Wordsworth
- Samuel Taylor Coleridge
- John Keats
- Christina Rossetti
- Elizabeth Barrett Browning

Beautiful moments or places

- Sunsets
- Twilight
- Deserted beaches
- City skylines
- Dawn chorus

Famous romances

- Romeo and Juliet
- Antony and Cleopatra
- Henry VIII and Anne Boleyn
- Pierre and Marie Curie
- Napoleon and Josephine
- King Edward VIII and Wallis Simpson

Beloved
Cherish
Everlasting
Intimacy
Blush
Tempestuous
Beguiling
Serenade

Coy
Furtive
Secret admirer
Engagement
Lovesick
Anticipation
Unrequited
Tenderness
Devotion
Desire
Clandestine
Melancholy
Tremulous
Affinity
Flirt
Implore

Feelings

Don't just describe X's feelings for Y. Show their intimacy through describing a tender moment or a simple gesture.

Special Delivery

Comedy words

Flummox

Bamboozle

Hullabaloo

Cantankerous

Blunderbuss

Taradiddle

Shenanigan

Skedaddle

Balderdash

Nincompoopery

Gunk

Ooze

Kerfuffle

Collywobbles

Brouhaha

Gobsmacked

Rumpus

Words

Don't litter your writing with too many crazy words. Use them sparingly and they'll have more impact.

Writing ideas

How to be funny

- Use unexpected similes and metaphors, e.g. as happy as a pig in a mud bath.

- Lead the reader to expect one thing... then add a surprise twist.

- Give your characters amusing things to say.

Spoonerisms

These are funny phrases where parts of words have been deliberately or accidentally switched over.

- Roaring with pain (pouring with rain)

- Nosey little cook (cosy little nook)

The words Shakespeare chose sound brilliant when they're spoken out loud.

"Away, you scullion! you rampallion! you fustilarian! I'll tickle your catastrophe."

[From Falstaff in *King Henry VI Part 2* by William Shakespeare]

Neologisms

If you can't find the word you want, make one up instead! Try combining several words, e.g. starmangler.

Fantasy words

How to start

Read fantasy stories

- Fairy tales
- Nordic sagas
- Myths and legends
- *The Lord of the Rings*

Create a new world

- What's its history?
- How does its society operate?
- Where are the key locations?
- Who are the inhabitants?
- How do they communicate?
- How advanced is the technology?

Borrow from history

Examples from history can enhance your fantasy world, whether it's a medieval joust, an Aztec sacrifice or a Roman invasion...

Fairy ring
Crystal ball
Demon
Dragon
Dwarf
Alchemy
Giant
Goblin
Gnome
Malevolence
Sage
Centaur

Oracle
Legend
Quest
Amulet
Kingdom
Elf
Pixie

Convince the reader

In fantasy and sci-fi stories, anything can happen... so long as you make the plot and the setting plausible. Create a convincing world where unbelievable things really could take place.

Ogre
Mischief

Realm
Talisman
Soothsayer

Sci-fi words

Alien

Time travel

Parallel universe

Android

Beam

Spaceship

Cyberspace

Telepathy

Dystopia

Matrix

Force field

Gravitation

Technology

Virtual

X-ray vision

Microbes

Meteors

Holographic

Extraterrestrial

Ray gun

Robot

Teleporting

Clone

Experiment

Innovation

Atomic

Futuristic

Revolutionary

Radical

Concept

Character tip

However alien your characters, make sure your readers can identify with them and understand their point of view.

Finding ideas

What if?

Science fiction is where hypothetical questions become reality, so keep asking yourself "What if...?"

Big issues

Use a fictional world to explore big, real-life issues, such as:

- Terrorism
- Pollution
- Overpopulation
- Globalization
- Superbugs

Other useful words

Starters

Try starting some of your sentences with these words or phrases.

Finally	Once upon a time	Every morning
Before long	There was once	By the time
Meanwhile	Long, long ago	Rarely
Coincidentally	For example	On the contrary
As if by magic	Whenever	Seldom have I
Although	No sooner	Perhaps
Astonishingly	Even though	In the past
Gradually	Eventually	Currently
Nevertheless	In particular	In the future

Linkers

These useful words can link together two parts of a sentence.

and	since	only if
or	given that	before
but	while	in case
nor	whether	provided that
so	when	then
yet	where	that
for	as long as	if
because	unless	
after	until	

Sentence linkers are called conjunctions.

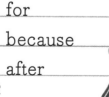

Other words for...

Vary your vocabulary by using some of these alternatives.

Use these alternatives sparingly – you don't want them to disrupt your dialogue.

Ran

sprinted	hurried	whizzed
bounded	dashed	bolted
raced	hared	sped
darted		

Said

badgered

croaked

declared

confessed

challenged

bragged

gasped

denied

jested

joked

pestered

snarled

blurted

nagged

commented

threatened

Looked

peered

glanced

examined

peeked

stared

glared

studied

glowered

observed

ogled

gaped

Thought

wondered

considered

brooded

reflected

imagined

contemplated

recalled

pondered

Asked

quizzed

demanded

requested

invited

queried

questioned

interrogated

93

Jottings

Use the following pages
for your own thoughts,
notes and ideas.

Six things you should
never tell your hamster

My
wish list

The
WORST
day ever

Index

Authors and poets

Acknowledgements

p.36 *Charlotte's Web* © E. B. White, first published by Harper and Brothers in 1952.

p.36 *1984* © George Orwell, first published by Secker and Warburg in 1949.

p.36 *The Hobbit* © J. R. R. Tolkien, published by George Allen Unwin in 1937.

p.45 "The Highwayman" © Alfred Noyes, first published in the August 1906 issue of *Blackwood's Magazine*.

p.45 *Peter and Wendy* (also known as *Peter Pan*) © Great Ormond Street Hospital, London. J. M. Barrie, first published by Hodder and Stoughton in 1911.

p.45 A letter to Frederick Lewis Allen (editor of *Harper's Magazine*) 7th May 1948 © Raymond Chandler

p.49 "A long time ago in a galaxy far, far away," from the opening of *Star Wars*, written and directed by George Lucas, 20th Century Fox.

p.56 "Poetry" © Marianne Moore, first published in the journal *Others* in 1919.

p.56 "A few words of a kind" © Dylan Thomas, speech recorded at Massachusetts Institute of Technology on 7th March, 1952.

p.56 "Poetry is like a bird, it ignores all frontiers." © Yevgeny Yevtushenko

p.65 "As I walked out one evening," W. H. Auden 1937. First published by Random House in *Another Time*. © 1940 W. H. Auden, renewed by the Estate of W. H. Auden.

p.74 *The Diaries of Samuel Pepys: A Selection*, edited by Robert Latham (Penguin Classics, paperback, 1st May 2003).

Credits and Quicklinks

Written by Katie Daynes
and Megan Cullis with advice
from Dr. Holly Linklater

Illustrated by Briony May Smith,
Lucile Gomez, Marie Mainguy
and Pep Boatella

Designed by Freya Harrison,
Laura Wood, Katie Webb
and Josephine Thompson

Edited by Ruth Brocklehurst

Usborne Quicklinks

For links to the websites
recommended in this book, go to
www.usborne.com/quicklinks
and type in the title of this book.
Please follow the internet
safety guidelines at the
Usborne Quicklinks website.

The websites recommended at Usborne Quicklinks are regularly reviewed but Usborne Publishing is not responsible and does not accept liability for the availability or content of any website other than its own, or for any exposure to harmful, offensive or inaccurate material which may appear on the Web.

Usborne Publishing will have no liability for any damage or loss caused by viruses that may be downloaded as a result of browsing the sites it recommends.

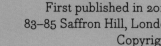

First published in 2017 by Usborne Publishing Ltd., Usborne House,
83–85 Saffron Hill, London, EC1N 8RT, United Kingdom. www.usborne.com
Copyright © 2017 Usborne Publishing Ltd.
The name Usborne and the devices are Trade Marks of Usborne Publishing Ltd.